The Art of

Characterization

**How to Use the Elements of Storytelling to
Connect Readers to an Unforgettable Cast**

DIRECTOR

FAY LAMB

The Art of Characterization: How to Use the Elements of
Storytelling to Connect Readers to an Unforgettable Cast

ISBN-13: 978-1-938092-50-3

ISBN-10: 1938092503

Published by Write Integrity Press, 130 Prominence Point
Pkwy. #130-330, Canton, GA 30114.

 www.WriteIntegrity.com

Printed in the United States of America.

Table of Contents

Introduction

Characters: You can't write a novel without them. A story's plot is all about the trouble a writer digs up for his characters.

During the course of this book, you're going to meet some of my favorite cast of scoundrels from my work *Pride Like Diamonds*, a love story about two master thieves, who, as you will see, find themselves in a bit of conflict.

Until I have a character firmly established in my imagination, I cannot begin to adequately tell his or her story. The emphasis here is on the word *adequately*. In order to have a character come to life, I must write and allow that character to introduce himself or herself to me. That's where the magic begins.

For writers, characters are real. They are flesh and blood, bone and sinew. They have personality and quirks. They are friends, and they are foe. They dance in the mind of an author, in a world the author has created for them.

The role of the writer is to make those characters come alive for his audience—the readers who pick up his novels.

When I was asked to teach three workshops over the summer, my preparation of those workshops began very early. I prayed over what I was to present because my ministry is to authors. I love to work, to teach, and to learn from other writers. God was faithful, as always, to turn on a light bulb inside my dim brain. When the lessons were clearly illuminated for me, I realized one important detail: as Solomon so aptly put it, there is nothing new under the sun.

Many books and classes have been presented on the

aspects of characterization, presenting ways to develop character, to match character traits, and even how to develop a character in an hour.

This book isn't one of those. I'm not going to talk about journaling or creating character outlines, but I also won't dissuade anyone from reading those works or practicing what they teach.

The purpose of this book is to present authors with a unique idea: use the other elements of storytelling to cast your novel with unforgettable characters. To do so, I'll be sharing examples from my aforementioned work, *Pride Like Diamonds.*

Before we delve in, let's take a look at the elements every storyteller should know and practice in order to bring craft to what they write. An expertise in craft will then help to bring vibrant characters to life.

The Art of Characterization

Chapter One
The Elements that Build a Story

The practice of certain writing techniques brings life and effervescence to our novels. Likewise, when the elements of storytelling are used as a whole, characters are brought to life in a way that attracts the reader to them and to their stories. Therefore, it only makes sense that when an author gains mastery over story elements, the characters become vibrant and the novel more enjoyable.

Grammar, Punctuation, and Spelling:

Yes, these are necessary elements of great storytelling.

A *New York Times* bestselling author once told me that she did not worry about punctuation, grammar, and spelling. Her job was to get the story written. A few years later, she decided to write an entirely different genre. To do so, she contracted with a small regional publisher. She's an excellent writer, and I enjoyed her newer genre; however, learning even a little about punctuation, grammar, and spelling might have saved her much embarrassment. The editing was atrocious.

A writer never knows when he'll find an editor who knows as little as he does. I've been very fortunate in my career to work with critique partners and editors who know their stuff. If an error gets by me in the publication of my work, I take full responsibility, because I have made it my business to know where a comma should be placed, how a word should be spelled, and what constitutes a grammatically correct sentence.

Besides, a working knowledge of grammar, punctuation, and spelling creates a professional presentation, and that's a plus when it comes to making a first impression on an editor or agent.

Characterization:

"Ah-ha," you might say. "This is what the book is about. Let's get down to business."

Characters are the heart of a novel. Without them

there are no emotions, no conflict, no message, and no need to tell a story. In 99.5% of all novels, a hero or heroine must be likeable from the start. In very rare occasions, main characters can start out doing something atrocious, but readers need to connect with them. This is why learning the art of characterization is vital to an author.

There are three important definitions for *character* that authors should know:

Merriam-Webster defines *character* as "the complex of mental and ethical traits marking and often individualizing a person."

In *Pride Like Diamonds,* both our hero, Drew Hallowell, and our heroine, Annie McGregor, have known only one way of life: thievery. Their mental and ethical traits spring from the only life they've ever known. Mentally, they are sharp and alert, but they think of their lives as thieves as survival—both in very different ways. Ethics for these two are not what most law-abiding citizens would think of principles. Drew and Annie have no problem stealing from others. However, ratting on someone in their trade is something they would never "ethically" do.

Another definition of *character* is "one of the

attributes or features that make up and distinguish an individual."

Drew is handsome, young, and sought after by the ladies, which is what he desires. Their attraction to him makes them easy marks. Annie uses her looks in a different way. Her father makes sure she's untouchable, but she knows how to make the men do whatever she needs them to do.

Character also means "a mark or distinctive quality."

Drew is street-wise and crafty. He's a professional pickpocket and thief. Annie and Drew are both legends among their respective unsavory peers. Both have been trained by their fathers in very different ways, but neither has ever been fingered for a crime.

Since this book is about characterization, and we are going to learn to use the other elements to our advantage in crafting unforgettable characters, let's look at those practices that will strengthen our prose.

Deep Point of View (DPOV):

Much of the information provided in this book includes deep point of view or DPOV. I have never been able to write in a simplistic POV where the only main objective is to stay with one character per scene without providing any depth to the character.

Deep POV is the essence of every story a reader declares he or she cannot put down. Deep POV immerses the reader into the head of the lead character through that character's actions, reactions, thoughts, experiences, and dialogue. Nothing should be experienced by the reader in a scene except through the lead character. We're going to discuss DPOV as we proceed, but let's continue to see what a deeper POV can do when used with other elements.

Showing versus Telling:

Despite the fact that we call what we do storytelling, an author must avoid telling his story. Instead, he wants to show his story to the reader, give the reader the experience of a movie inside the reader's head.

When done correctly, the use of DPOV eliminates unnecessary telling narrative. How does DPOV do this? It erases the need for words such as *he saw*, *she heard, he thought, he realized*, and other similar phrases that place the reader on the outside of the story looking in. Deep POV also eliminates needless adverbs in dialogue tags by putting the reader inside the lead character's head and showing the reader how and why the character reacts the way he does.

The proper use of DPOV also eliminates the tendency to throw in a dump load of back story and description. Deep POV allows an author to bring in only the information necessary, and when it is brought in through the lead character's thoughts and dialogue, the result is a story that moves forward and not backward. A story does not turn into a transporter, taking the reader from the present and dropping them into the past. Nor does the story stop to provide every detail about a scene. Instead, only important information is relayed through our lead character.

Conflict:

Any author who says conflict is not a necessary part of storytelling is an author who will not soon find publication. A novel without conflict is a look at someone walking through life without a care in the world.

Who wants to read a story like that?

No one.

Conflict does not have to come externally in the form of explosions, sadistic villains, or total destruction of life. A good war or words between sisters is a great showing of external conflict. Likewise, internal conflict can be as *explosive* as a man contemplating suicide or as subtle as fear in the heart of a woman when she's unsure if her husband is having an affair. Good external and internal conflicts escalate as the story progresses.

Conflict matches the genre and the story. For instance, a formulaic contemporary romance is not going to hold the tension of a romantic thriller. Instead, the conflict will be a lighter tension between the hero and heroine.

Write it down: a scene without conflict is an unnecessary addition to your work.

Dialogue:

Like conflict, dialogue is necessary. Readers tend to skip over large blocks of paragraphing. Unconsciously, they look for those double quotation marks. Why? Because dialogue is truly the meat of the scene. Through pertinent dialogue, a reader receives the message, gets to the heart of the conflict, and learns more about the unfolding plot.

Notice I said *pertinent.* In real life, we have time for the niceties. In fiction, all words spoken by the characters should lend something to the plot.

Now, let's allow the characters from *Pride Like Diamonds* to come on stage and show how these elements we've just discussed can create an unforgettable cast.

Chapter Two

Deep POV, The Author/Director's Camera Lens

Characters are always on stage in my imagination. For a very long time, I had no idea that not all people tell themselves stories, interact with characters, or even fall asleep devising plots for the characters that live in their brain. Then one day I said something about a work in progress. My husband cast me a glance that said he thought I was completely out of my mind.

"What? You don't tell yourself stories?" I asked.

He shook his head. "No."

I thought on that for a long while and then I asked, "If you don't have stories running through your mind, what do you think about?"

He really couldn't give me an acceptable answer.

My mind would have a vacancy sign hanging inside if my characters left residence. I'd go mad. I have always been entertained by my make-believe friends. They are my reality.

Often, my characters audition for me, or they sit across the table from me, and they share their stories. As the director, I decide on which characters need to be cast for my work in progress.

I'll get away from the director's chair for a while to devise the plot, but when I sit down to write, the author's cap comes off. I take on the role of director.

Deep POV becomes my director's camera lens, and through it unfolds the story for my readers. The camera lens I use is much more powerful than any developed for Hollywood. The deep POV camera lens gives me the ability to do something that no Hollywood director can draw from a shot, no matter how wide or close up. My camera lens provides the psyche of my POV character. At all times, my readers can know exactly what that character is thinking (even if the thoughts are incorrect).

Deep POV comes to the reader through the lead character. If I'm writing in first person, the camera is always my first person POV character. This eliminates internal monologue with the exception of prayer and a sparing use to emphasize important thought. When writing in third-person limited, my camera lens is the lead for the scene I'm writing.

In order to get the most out of the use of DPOV, two things must be done:

First, when utilizing DPOV, it is always best to begin each scene—yes, I said each scene—by providing the POV character with the lead action, thought, or experiences. In other words, set your stage. Notice, though, that I didn't suggest starting the scene with the POV character's dialogue. Sure, it can be done, but starting dialogue as the first line of a scene is like having a talking head without a body. It's a dangerous practice. Do it carefully. Do it correctly.

After setting the stage, every bit of information in the scene comes through the dialogue, thought, action, and reaction of the point-of-view character. This is how we eliminate those telling phrases mentioned above.

To emphasize the camera lens with a psyche, here's a scene from the viewpoint of the overall villain in *Pride*

The Art of Characterization

Like Diamonds.

Feagan followed behind the young man—his boy—as he meandered through the hustling crowds on Broadway. Dodger thought he could get away from him by moving out of the slums where Feagan had left him. Feagan would let his son think that way. Dodger and his brother would soon learn who controlled their moves.

Wolf McGregor would learn as well.

Life was a chess game, and sometimes the matches went on for years. The king was in his sights. Feagan just had to utilize his pawns effectively, move them into place, let McGregor take them off the board. That's all he needed for checkmate.

Dodger picked up pace, and Feagan matched the stride, careful to stay behind, but not far enough that he couldn't watch the boy's next move. Dodger lowered his arm to his side and with the sleight of hand Feagan had taught him from a tender age, Dodger pulled the wallet from the back pocket of the man strolling beside him. The man didn't move, didn't react. Never caught on.

Dodger strolled past the mark, turning to offer the man a smile. "Good day," he said.

Feagan had tried to beat the arrogance out of his

youngest son, but now, it made Feagan smile.

"Henry Atwell!" a man called.

Feagan turned and planted a smile on his face. "Wolf, what a pleasure to see you up so early on a Monday morning."

Wolf looked beyond him. "Was that Drew Hallowell?"

"Why, yes. Yes, it was. The little beggar lifted a wallet."

Wolf didn't respond, but he continued to look to where the young man had disappeared into the crowd.

Feagan, Dodger, Ollie, all legends on the streets of New York. No one knew their real identities, and even his sons had never learned his. They knew him only as Feagan.

"That boy has promise," Wolf said.

Checkmate was definitely in Feagan's future.

Do you get the idea that you're in the mind of a somewhat psychotic criminal—one who uses his own sons for his own gain, one who is living out a fantasy from a Charles Dickens' novel? The camera lens allowed us to see Feagan's world, both the street that he's walking down, the young man he's following, and the inner workings of a brain that just isn't quite right. Also, we get a hint that *Pride Like Diamonds* is going to have some twists and turns.

Okay, it's time to take off your author's cap and sit in your director's chair. Let's allow some other characters to take the stage and bring with them, as their props, other elements of storytelling.

Chapter Three

Bringing Characters on Stage

When we set our stage, we do several things with our first paragraph.

We give our lead character the first action. Caution. The action given to the character needs to be something that adds to the scene. For that reason, an author must decide who has the most to win or lose in a chosen scene. The character with the most at stake for that scene is your POV character.

Also, when necessary, we set time and place for our

scene, and we let the reader know who is in the scene with our characters. Doing so prevents the reader from feeling as if characters suddenly drop from the cosmos into the scene.

In this example from *Pride Like Diamonds*, Wolf McGregor, makes his entrance:

Wolf McGregor straightened his tie and buttoned his suit jacket then descended the mahogany stairs. He checked his ruby cufflinks. His daughter, Annie, would no doubt tell him at some point in the evening that his age was showing. No one wore cufflinks these days, but he enjoyed the elegance of the costly gems.

Just as Feagan/Henry's initial actions established him as our POV character in the last scene, Wolf's do the same here. Notice, also, like Feagan/Henry, Wolf wasn't given any old action.

In one sentence, a picture of a wealthy man is provided to the reader. A poorer man might be dressed in a suit and tie, but would he have a mahogany staircase? If that didn't quite get the reader's attention, Wolf's next action (checking his ruby cufflinks) and his thoughts about the cufflinks drive the point home.

Chapter Four
Scene Description, A Character's Job

With Wolf firmly on the stage and his POV set, we move on to the description of our scene. A director knows everything possible about the stage on which his cast will bring life to the story. Likewise, an author should have the setting firmly in mind.

This does not mean the reader must be regaled with a description of every square inch of the setting. Instead, an author should show (and not tell) what is important to that scene through the eyes of the POV character. To do this, avoid telling the reader about the floral chair in the corner, unless that floral chair has importance.

Bringing on the important props helps our description work double duty. In showing what is important to the lead character, we build that character for the audience.

Authors are lousy at description. We tend to want to over describe, thinking the reader needs help. Readers' imaginations need room to envision the setting on their own, and that's the importance of only showing the necessary details. That's why description is the job for your POV character.

Let's take a look beyond Wolf's mahogany stairs to find out what is important to him. The stage has already been set with Wolf as our POV character. Now, we're moving on.

His daughter was usually the first one ready for an important night. He took her delay as a sign that she was serious about her assignment. Wolf sat on the Queen Anne sofa and looked up at the life-size portrait of his best creation. The painting hung over his white marble fireplace. He might be a little biased, but Wolf knew quality. His daughter was the most beautiful woman he'd ever known. She was the finest master thief New York would never know.

His gaze moved to the gilded frame on the opposite wall. Oh, the picture in the front of the frame was worth a fortune. The painting behind it, however, was of innumerable worth. With it, Annie had proven she'd learned all he had to teach her.

Tonight, though, he'd charged her with stealing a different kind of treasure ... a young man's heart.

This scene, described through the POV character, tells just as much about Wolf as it does his living room, doesn't it?

What is important to this wealthy man?

His daughter, Annie? He has a life-size portrait of her over his fireplace.

But is she valuable to him because he loves her or for another reason?

Notice, I didn't describe Annie. Wolf knows his daughter. He's going to think of her as beautiful without recounting her features. Nope, we're going to leave that description for someone else—someone who has a reason to recount Annie's looks.

What else do you learn about Wolf?

He's a master thief, and he's groomed his daughter to follow in his crooked footsteps.

Through Wolf's POV what do we know about the skills of his daughter, another character in the story? Annie hasn't even stepped onto the stage, but we know, wow, she's pretty good at thievery.

Here our stage is set, and our description has worked double duty.

But what about the descriptions of our characters?

Chapter Five

Mirror, Mirror on the Wall: Character Description

Writing character descriptions seems to give many writers trouble.

Again, as with scenery, an author should never stop a story to tell the reader what his characters look like.

POV characters should never intentionally describe themselves, either. I've seen it many times. A woman looks in the mirror and thinks about her looks—and they're always about her beauty. That builds your character, but not in the way you desire—unless your character is an evil queen in a fairytale.

Not many women look into a mirror and see things they are happy with, and ones who think about themselves in that way are kind of, let's say, vain. And any man who stares in the mirror and thinks of such things does not a hero make.

Character descriptions come primarily from <u>other</u> POV characters or natural events that make it plausible for the character to mention something about his or her own looks.

Most readers create a picture of the hero or heroine in their own minds, and if you asked them what they thought your character looked like, most times, it isn't going to be anything like you imagined your character. So, why, unless you have a very good reason, would you want to try to describe every square inch of the character? Just as with scene descriptions, leave something to the readers' imaginations. Also, as with the scenery, make the description you provide work twice as hard.

In the following example, our lead character is Wolf's daughter, Annie McGregor. She's just met an irresistible man. Listen carefully to Annie's deep POV. I think you'll see that her description of him tells us much more about her that she realizes. In this scene, we're coming into the middle of it, so imagine that the scene has already been set. This is the pertinent portion I want you to see:

So that's why Poppa didn't have a problem with her talking to Drew Hallowell. He was the man Poppa set as her mark. Why then did she feel like a piece of bait dangling between these two men? She shook the mutinous thought away. Her father wouldn't put her in danger. She was his most valuable asset. He'd said that enough.

She circled the pool, keeping a steady gaze on Drew, drawing him in.

Not a tall drink of water. His under six foot height complimented Annie's 5'6" frame.

There was something raw and attractive about his wispy brown strands that seemed to settle anywhere on his head that they wished. A touch of an overbite kept him from appearing too perfect, like a cardboard cutout of a Ken doll. No, he wasn't perfect. Perfection was for diamonds and paintings by Rembrandt. Not men.

But it wasn't Drew Hallowell's good looks alone that captured her attention. Across the shimmering lights in the water, he stared in her direction before starting her way. He bore a look about him of danger, as if he lived life on the edge. All evening, his coffee-colored eyes had worn a façade of calm composure. He kept something under control, but Annie was too afraid to discover what.

A genuine smile reached his eyes. Still she didn't completely trust him.

He was hot—like the diamond she'd lifted from the counter of Tiffany's.

"Me watch is telling me your coach should arrive any moment now, Cinderella, else it will turn into a pumpkin at the stroke of midnight."

And his British accent only completed the package.

Okay, we learn that Wolf McGregor's beautiful daughter is 5'6" tall. That's the obvious physical detail, which comes across in a natural thought—Annie comparing her height to his—but what else does Annie reveal about herself in this passage that is supposedly about her description of Drew Hallowell?

She reveals that she might just have a trust issue with Wolf—maybe for the first time. She feels vulnerable (like bait).

We know from Wolf's POV that his daughter is a master thief. Here we have further evidence that Annie isn't just a kleptomaniac or a petty criminal. Only a master thief could lift a diamond from the counter of Tiffany's without getting caught. But that just shows us she's good at what she does.

What about her perception of Drew as imperfect— her belief that perfection is for diamonds and artistic masterpieces? Do you think maybe she's known some cold men in her life? Or maybe the men in her life—like her father—value diamonds and paintings over relationships? Maybe Annie is looking for a man who cares more about her than about her skills as a thief?

Then there's the fact that though she's a master thief, this man's looks scream danger. I'd think the life of a master thief would be pretty dangerous. She also knows Drew is putting up a front. She sees the façade of calm composure in his eyes.

She's also afraid to find out what he's keeping under control. This brings up a myriad of questions about her and this man. Is she used to being mistreated and afraid that he will do the same?

Or maybe—just maybe—she sees a little of herself in Drew Hallowell, and she has an inkling that he's a thief who's already stolen her heart with his British accent and all of the things they have in common.

And though we're in Annie's POV, what does Drew's single line of dialogue tell you about what he knows about Annie? Wasn't Cinderella, in some ways, an imposter? But Annie hears the accent and not the words. You, the reader, hear the words.

Can you see where this description worked double duty to share insight into both the POV character and her hero and put vibrancy in their being?

Chapter Six

The Vibrant Trio of Dialogue, Thought, and Action

There is a trio of story elements that, when used correctly, bring vibrancy to our characters.

Dialogue relays relevant information between characters that is important to the scene. Distinctive dialogue is a part of our characters.

The thought (through deep POV) adds a little more insight into the *mindset* of the POV character, draws the reader into the scene, and helps bring about natural description.

Action adds more insight into the character—

especially unique actions.

To demonstrate the effectiveness of the vibrant trio, let's meet Drew through his deep POV and at the same time get a little description of Annie from our hero. Up until this time we've seen mostly thought and action, but let's see what adding a touch of dialogue brings to our characters.

Drew walked into the flat and kicked the door closed.

"How'd it go?" His older brother looked away from the sixty-inch telly. The Knicks were playing tonight. "You better not tell me I missed this game for nothing."

"Enough about the game, Benny. I've heard it for three days now." Drew had sold the tickets that, by chance, earlier in the week, he'd lifted from a wallet along with a hundred dollars. They'd planned to attend the game together. If security had approached them about the seats, they'd just claim they bought a $300 pencil from a guy off the street. That pencil just happened to come with the tickets. They'd never get Drew for a petty crime. If he ever got caught, it would be for something worth doing time. But that was beside the point. They'd missed the game to allow Drew to attend a dinner party. Some things were just more important than basketball.

Like getting into Wolf McGregor's good graces and moving up in the world.

"I had meself a good night. A very good night." He plopped down on the old couch and kicked his shoes off before stretching his legs out on the unfashionable antique table they'd found at Goodwill. He smiled. He couldn't help himself.

"Yeah," Benny nodded, "looks like you had a great time. But did you get the job done?"

Drew closed his eyes and allowed a vision to play in his memory, a vision of blonde curls—strands he'd wanted to push behind Annie McGregor's delicate shoulder just to feel the silkiness between his fingers—and her eyes of blue—like a perfectly cut pair of sapphires whose brilliance shone in the lights of Harriet Tyndale's old New York mansion.

"Annie McGregor was easier to get close to than I thought. What a looker, that one." He gave a whistle of approval. If he wasn't careful, he'd let his guard down. He'd tried all night to keep his passion under control. "She might be the first girl to win me heart—if I let her."

Ben sat up. "Keep your head in the game." He stared at Drew until the roaring crowd on the television gained his attention.

"Yeah. Yeah. You know I will. But there's a reason her old man is so overprotective. He has a gorgeous daughter and a valuable asset." Still, no one came close to having Drew's sleight of hand, his ability to con the hardest soul, and the daring to pull off some masterful thievery—not even his brother. That's why this was his game. And he would win.

"One thing. I need to score a ticket to Wicked for next Saturday's performance, even if I have to buy it."

"To take the girl?" Ben leaned forward.

Drew laughed. "No. She's after me mark, and I plan to keep her from getting her. Can't let one of me gals steal from the other one now, can I? I'll be at that show, and I'll take Ms. Tyndale off Annie's hands."

The gorgeous little blonde would have to admit to her father that she'd lost to Drew ... and then maybe Wolf would consider letting Drew—and Ben—in on what Drew had heard would be the biggest heist in years.

He reached into his suit pocket. Empty. He stood and patted his back pocket. Nothing.

"You lose something?" Ben yawned.

"Yeah." Drew smiled. "Me wallet's gone missing. Imagine that." His contingency plan was firmly in place.

"Imagine that." Ben tossed a musty couch pillow at

him and winked. "You're the best, little brother. The best."

Yeah, he was. And getting to know Annie McGregor was going to be a lot of fun.

Just as in our scenes with Wolf and Annie, we learn things about Drew without Drew telling us. He shows us his world. Did you notice the bit of back story in that third paragraph? If you didn't, I'm happy about it, but if you caught it, do you understand why I added it?

I wanted Drew to show you that he—and maybe his brother—are wily street thieves. The wallet that Feagan watched Drew lift not only had money. It also had tickets to a Knicks game. Drew planned to attend that game despite the fact that the authorities might check on two men sitting in the seats of a ticketholder who reported his tickets stolen. Drew had a plan ... a crafty plan.

Not only is Drew a wily street thief, he's a poor one. The only thing of value in Drew's "flat" and notice that he used a term that someone from the UK would use, is a pretty large "telly" (another UK term). Everything else that Drew shows us is old, unfashionably antique, and musty.

Another point about his dialogue. Drew has a

distinctive way of speaking. He uses *me* in the place of *my*. Drew doesn't have to spill a lot of dialect. This little change in speech tells us not only that Drew is a Brit. It also tells us that he and Ben most likely have a working-class British heritage.

With a combination of thought and dialogue, we also see that Drew is taken by Ms. McGregor. His thoughtful description shows us this, but in dialogue he lets it slip that he's more than a little interested in her. That is until Ben reacts to the truth.

That brings on a touch of conflict. Notice that any further information about his feelings for Annie comes through his thoughts. Chastised by Ben, Drew keeps the information to himself. But Benny's warning isn't the only hint of conflict. Drew's thoughts about the beautiful blonde are already contradictory. She's a mark—or is she? He can tell himself that, but Drew reveals to us who the real mark is for him.

It's Annie's father who is apparently planning some great heist, and Drew and Ben want to be invited to take part. Annie is the key. Do you get the idea that her premonition of herself as the bait is real?

And what about Drew's wallet? Would someone who easily picks pockets allow someone to pick his? That alone tells us that Drew planned for Annie to take his wallet to open the door for him to see her again— if his plan failed.

All of this information comes through the vibrant trio of dialogue, thought, and action.

One more question. Do you see that everyone is playing this game, and each of the men believe they're in control?

What about Annie? Is she in control or is she being controlled?

The Art of Characterization

Chapter Seven

Conflict: The Driving Force for Characterization

We saw a hint of this next element in our last example, but let's bring it front and center now. Conflict is the force that drives our plots. If you have a conflict-free plot, you don't have a story.

Characters are made for conflict, and here's why:

❖ Characters are pushed to their limits when they face conflict.

❖ In situations of intense conflict, characters are forced to meet challenges in ways they might not expect.

❖ As with everything else we've learned, the

strength of conflict is in proportion to the depths that we can immerse our readers into the story.

❖ The actions our characters take to resolve their conflicts is what draws a reader to them.

Conflict, like everything else we have discussed, should be brought to us through our characters. Let's see what a little bit of conflict infused with dialogue, action, and thoughts will do to draw our readers to our hero and our heroine, Drew and Annie.

Drew wiped the sweat from his brow and looked around the room.

Annie stood beside him. Her shirt was drenched, but he'd been amazed at her ability to scale a building. Spiderwoman, she was.

He only hoped she'd been half as impressed with his ability to cut through the glass without triggering the sensitive alarm.

That was behind them now. This was the most dangerous part of the job. They were inside. Trapped if they made one wrong move.

He looked around the room of framed art. Something wasn't right. The plans—the ones Wolf had been so adamant about them using—showed the vault location here in this wing. Ben had cased the home without Wolf's knowledge. Ben swore the floor plan Wolf gave them was wrong.

Benny just might have been right.

"Drew," Annie whispered against his ear, the sound as soft as a feather cutting through air. "Where is it?"

He shook his head.

Her fingers laced through his. Her body trembled.

Whatever was happening, she wasn't in on it. This wasn't a setup to eliminate him and Ben from the heist and the payout. Not unless Wolf was willing to sacrifice his daughter for the prize. Drew didn't think so.

"Maybe it's behind one of the paintings." The warmth of her touch left him.

"Annie, no!" He reached out for her, his harsh, low tone coming too late.

She breached the laser he'd known was there. The alarm pierced the air.

She spun toward him, blue eyes wide. "We have to go."

Cut and run. He knew how to do that. For him, it had always been an act of self-preservation. Why now wouldn't his feet carry him out of the danger? Because he wasn't sure if he could get Annie out, too.

"Please!" Annie tugged at him.

Drew shook his head and nodded toward the door.
Annie whirled to face the truth ... a large security guard
with a small but powerful gun.

Drew yanked Annie back toward him, his forearm
under her neck. "I told you what would happen if I got
caught!" he snarled. "Now, you're going to pay."

Annie struggled in his grasp.

"Let her go, man. A hostage only makes it worse.
There's no way out of this." The guard leveled the gun.

"Hostage—"

Drew tightened his hold on her, strangling Annie's
counter to the guard's assumption. Then he threw her
toward the man and raised his hands. If he was lucky,
she'd get out of this, and he wouldn't get shot. Keeping
her safe was worth any time he'd do in prison. If she'd
only keep her mouth shut.

The guard moved behind Drew, pulling his hands
down and slipping the cuffs on in one fluid motion.
"Smart move, son."

A sound lifted from the open hall. Hands coming
together as if someone enjoyed a good show.

Wolf stepped into view. "Drew, my boy. Brilliant.

Annie is always my first priority. I'm glad she's yours. Now, we can truly get to work." Wolf clasped the security guard on the shoulder. "Thanks, Richard, for allowing us to use your resources for training."

"Anything for my five percent cut." Richard laughed and released Drew from his confines. "Look at the kid. He's white as chalk on a blackboard."

Of course he was. Annie could have been killed. Accidents happened in tense situations.

Drew looked into her blue eyes. The sapphires were clouded with tears.

As Wolf stepped toward his daughter, she raised her hand. The man took an open handed slap.

Drew stepped in front of Annie, shielding her from the older man's retaliation. If Drew had even threatened to raise a hand to his old man, he wouldn't expect to live through Feagan's reaction.

"I'm done!" Annie screamed and countered his protection by moving around Drew, blocking him from Wolf's reach. "Do you hear me? You're playing a dangerous game, and that's fine as long as I'm the only one in danger." She straightened, her height almost matching her father's.

Drew touched her blonde curls, damp from the sweat

of exertion and most likely fear. He pulled her backward, nestling her into his arms.

She still trembled.

He hadn't known she cared. "I'm okay, Annie. Nothing like a good scare to make sure you're more cautious the next time."

Ben had told Drew he thought this was a test of ability or loyalty. Next time Ben had a hunch, Drew would listen. Whatever this had been, he was sure he'd won the loyalty of the father and the heart of the daughter.

Still, he hated the look of utter disillusionment on Annie's face.

The apparent conflict in this scene is the fact that they are trapped in a location that screams trouble for Drew—and we see through Drew's POV that Annie feels the same way, but do you see the other forms of conflict that come out through Drew's deep POV?

Drew's brother warned him, and Drew hadn't listened—or had he?

Through Drew's POV do you see Annie's nervousness? She's a master thief. She's been through this before. Why then does she make a serious blunder? Drew doesn't understand this, but through what he shows the reader, do you get the idea that she's worried for him in the same way he's worried about her?

Annie's conflict with her father is seen through Drew's eyes, and he tries to soothe the situation, but by the end of the scene, do you get the feeling that Drew took a gamble without really knowing how it would play out? If Benny had been right, Wolf would be playing into Drew's hands, but if the heist had been real and everything had gone wrong, Drew would have been sent away for a very long time.

Drew doesn't have to tell you that he loves Annie. He showed it. Remember the scene in Drew's flat. What did he say? If he got caught, it would be for something worth doing time. For Drew, Annie has become that something.

In contrast to Wolf's behavior, who do you believe loves Annie more, Drew or Wolf?

And one more thing—this disillusionment on Annie's face, do you think it could be the start of new conflict that might just bring a new way of life to our hero and heroine?

The Art of Characterization

Chapter Eight

Using the Elements of Storytelling Effectively

So, there you have it. The secret formula for connecting your readers to your characters isn't some new formula to develop characterization. The key isn't something separate from the other elements we're learning. Character building is enhanced by a strengthening and deepening of point of view.

When deep point of view is used to its utmost, telling falls away from our prose, and the movie screen inside the reader's head begins to flash with vibrant scenery and action. The camera lens delivers the reader into the psyche of the lead character, and the reader stays there until he places the book down.

Essential back story and other information that would normally stop the camera from rolling is eliminated. Instead, the information is layered in when necessary through the deep point of view of the main character, through his reactions to and experiences with other characters, and through his own thoughts. Such actions bring the character alive for the author's audience.

Motivating conflict between the point-of-view character and others in the cast reaches out and keeps the reader engaged in the story.

Begin to develop a knowledge of this amazing tool called deep POV and use it to strengthen every element of writing fiction.

Never stop practicing because in practice true art is found.

Chapter Nine

An Exercise in Writing Characters

Now, let's cast some characters. I'm presenting you with the information from a scene from one of my future releases. This is a scene I enjoyed writing, and I thought it would be fun for you to create your own stage in which this could happen.

Here's the info you'll need:

Characters' Names: A husband and wife (you name your characters).

Location: The couple's kitchen. She's cooking dinner. He's keeping a wary eye on her.

Description: Whatever you think is important for the scene.

Conflict: He doesn't know this, but she has just learned she's pregnant. This is something they've been looking forward to. Trouble is, returning from the doctor's office, she saw him with another woman—a woman he should not have been with. He has just learned from the other woman that she, too, is pregnant with his child. His two worlds collide when his wife tells him both pieces of news: she's pregnant, and she saw him with the other woman.

There we have it: character, location, action, description (I'm sure you have a picture in your mind), and conflict. Now, let's ask some questions to help with your crafting of the scene the way that you see it. There aren't any right or wrong answers. Yeah, I've already written my scene. It's in a novel that will be published, but I have no fear in sharing this with you because I can guarantee you that none of our scenes are going to look alike.

Question #1: Who should be our POV character? Think about it. Who, in your opinion, has the most to win or lose in this scene?

_____

_____

_____

_____

_____

_____

_____

_____

Question #2: With our POV character in place, what description and props in this location are important for the POV character to bring into the scene?

_____

_____

_____

_____

_____

_____

_____

_____

_____

Question #3: What about the other character is important for the POV character to note?

_____

_____

_____

_____

_____

_____

_____

Question #4: How can you use dialogue, action, and thought to bring home the powerful conflict of the scene and bring vibrancy to their character?

_____

_____

_____

_____

_____

_____

_____

_____

_____

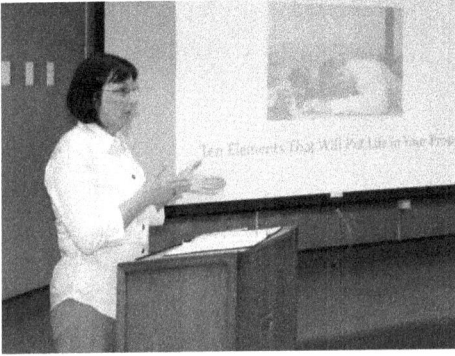

About the Author

Fay Lamb is an acquisition editor for a Christian publisher. She also provides freelance fiction edits. Fay loves to work with authors, and she is known as the Tactical Editor on Facebook where she offers practical advice for self-editing and interacts with readers on a wide range of questions and concerns.

Fay's emotionally charged novels remind the reader that God is always in the details. Fay has contracted with Write Integrity Press for three separate series in three different genres.

Fay motivates authors with her workshops on the elements of storytelling. She is a past-secretary for American Christian Fiction Writers. Past President of the Central Florida chapter of American Christian Fiction Writer's. She served for four years as the moderator for ACFW's critique group, Scribes.

Visit Fay on the Web:
www.FayLamb.com

Other Books by Fay Lamb

Available on Amazon, Kindle, and by request from most local booksellers

Amazing Grace Series

Stalking Willow
Available Now!

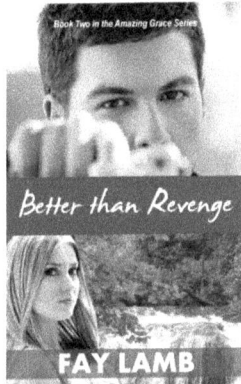

Better than Revenge
October 2013!

Others Coming 2014!

Ties that Bind Series

Charisse
Available Now!

Libby October 2013, *Hope* and *Delilah* ~ 2014

Look for other books

published by

www.WriteIntegrity.com

and

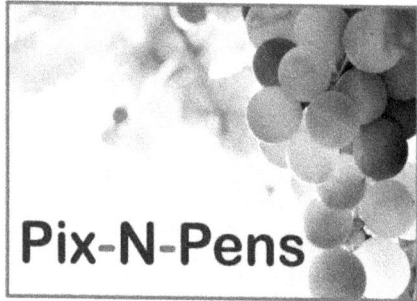

Pix-N-Pens Publishing

www.PixNPens.com

www.ingramcontent.com/pod-product-compliance
Lightning Source LLC
Chambersburg PA
CBHW071724290326
41933CB00051B/2084